Making Disciples for the Workplace
How to Nurture Whole-life Discipleship

Mark Greene
Mission Champion, LICC

GROVE BOOKS LIMITED
RIDLEY HALL RD CAMBRIDGE CB3 9HU

Contents

'Your ordinary contact with God takes place where your fellow men, your yearnings, your work and your affections are. There you have your daily encounter with Christ. It is in the midst of the most material things of the earth that we must sanctify ourselves, serving God and all mankind.'
'Heaven and earth seem to merge, my children, on the horizon. But where they really meet is in your hearts, when you sanctify your everyday lives...'
St Josemaría Escrivá, founder of Opus Dei[1]

'It [becoming a nun] was the only thing I wanted because
I didn't know there were other ways to love God completely.
I now know of course that you can be a bus conductress
or a television person and love God completely.'
Sister Wendy Beckett[2]

Acknowledgments
With thanks to Team LICC and the many workers and church leaders
who have helped distill this learning over the years.

First Impression October 2021
ISSN 2753-9369
ISBN 978 1 78827 197 4

Work in an Uncertain World

The Joy of Working with God

> Last Sunday morning I was calling out to God for some solutions to the problems I was facing in my work. Those problems were really worrying me, disturbing me. A few hours later in the morning service, when Kim was sharing her testimony about how God had helped her in her job as a pharmacist, I heard these words: 'God wants to be part of our work.' I was shocked because at that moment I really felt that those words were addressed to me personally. And when after a few seconds the minister again said, 'God wants to be part of our work,' I felt relief in my spirit about my work. It was a miracle for me. I physically felt how trouble and worry left me and instead my heart was filled with real peace.
>
> You know, I didn't receive specific answers to my specific questions, although that would have been a great victory in the battle about my work, but God did better. He taught me, 'I want to be a part of your job.' And this became a victory for me in a whole war, not just one battle. Now I know God is part of my work.
>
> Oleg Lakovenko, CEO and founder of PRCOM, a marketing agency[3]

Relief, joy, peace, purpose.

That is what happens when God's people know that God cares about their daily work. That is what happens when they realize that their work is an arena for their discipleship—a context to learn and live the way of Jesus, day by working day. Indeed, is there any reason why Christ's promise to be with his people would not apply in the workplace? Is there any reason why Christ, the master disciple-maker, would waste such a rich opportunity to work through his people, and to teach, correct, rebuke, train, empower, grow and mature his followers in character and impact, for his glory? Is there any reason why Christ would not want his people take up their cross daily at work and to seek his face, his wisdom, his grace for their work, their workplace and their work colleagues?

Vitally, relief, joy, peace and purpose in daily work are not just important to Christians. They are important to every human being on the face of the planet.

The gospel is good news for work, workplaces, and workers. And the good news about work is vital for our mission. Dorothy L Sayers, the novelist, playwright, and Christian apologist, put it this way:

> In nothing has the church so lost her hold on reality as her failure to understand and respect the secular vocation. She has allowed work and religion to become separate departments, and is astonished to find that, as a result, the secular work of the world is turned to purely selfish and destructive ends, and that the greater part of the world's intelligent workers have become irreligious or at least uninterested in religion...But is it astonishing? How can anyone remain interested in a religion which seems to have no concern with nine-tenths of his life?[4]

Sayers' point was not just about work—her point was about the gospel. And it applies today. The failure to teach work well is part of a wider failure to offer a whole-life gospel to non-believers. No wonder people are not gripped by the gospel. The gospel we present rarely includes any compelling vision for the transformation of ordinary daily life. And this is particularly important for 18-to-35-year-olds who do not want to live a compartmentalized life, to be one person on Tuesday and someone different on Saturday or Sunday. They are seeking an integrated, authentic life of purpose that includes their work. They want everything to count. And, of course, in Christ it does. It is just that the vast majority of God's people do not know that yet. Globally.

Actually, my sense is that the vast majority of Christians—those not in church-paid work—actually believe that their work is less important to God than the work of a church leader or overseas missionary. They see themselves as second-class Christians. Not surprisingly, perhaps, since they are unlikely to have had their choice to go into HR or coding or bricklaying tested and affirmed by their local church. And they are unlikely to have been proactively supported and regularly prayed for by their fellow believers in that work. Yes, all Christians are equal, but some Christians are more equal than others.

Of course, this is not intentional. Indeed, you would be hard-pressed to find many church leaders who would argue that God is not interested in all of life. But it is one thing to know something and quite another to create a way of being church that reflects that reality.

However, when God's truth about work sets people free, it feels like a second conversion. And it leads to a life of greater joy in Christ and much greater fruitfulness for him—working day by working day. Importantly, as we painfully emerge from the damage and disruption wrought by COVID-19 into what will no doubt be a different working world, we as God's people have a particular opportunity to help shape what that might look like.

Work in Crisis

> Without work, all life goes rotten.
> But when work is soulless, life stifles and dies.
>
> Albert Camus

Work. It is central to the flourishing of individuals and nations worldwide.

And yet, over the last five hundred years, it has been an area for which we, as the church, have struggled to envision and empower God's people. Our often thin response to work represents a tragic loss not only for Christians but for their co-workers, the organizations they serve, the communities they are part of and the countries they live in. The Bible has a vision for what good working looks like. And, worldwide, most work does not look like it.

Even before the pandemic, the future of work had been looking bleak, with an alarming rise in the number of people in vulnerable work that might not be there for very long: 40% of Europeans, 80% globally. Similarly, psychologists had already made the frankly predictable connection between the burgeoning gig economy and declines in emotional and mental well-being. Economists had warned that the combination of AI, robotics and hypercomputers mining-mining-mining humongous quantities of data would usher in a new industrial revolution that could consign any prospect of full employment to the realm of fantasy fiction. And there was concern about the overvaluing of 'head' work over 'hand' work or 'heart' work: that is, the overvaluing, and therefore relative over-rewarding, of knowledge workers as opposed to people who work with their hands or whose work focuses on nurture, healing and care.

Already there was concern about continuing unequal pay and opportunity for women, and the outrageous inequality in the employment prospects of ethnic minorities. Indeed, nationally and globally, injustice abounds—grim working conditions, poverty-line pay, squeezing of suppliers, just-legal but unjust corporate tax contributions in some sectors, suppression of trade unions. The pandemic has highlighted these realities—as well as a whole range of generational, regional, national and global inequalities—and it has accelerated, in the West at least, much higher levels of remote working, with economic and psychological consequences that are only just emerging. We may have all been in the same storm, but we have not been in the same boat.

In such turbulent and uncharted waters, we surely have a responsibility to our Lord and our world to ensure that God's people have the biblical frame-works and the spiritual practices that will enable them to bring his wisdom and ways to the practice of work—whether that is in Preston or Sao Paulo, in a field of maize, an office, a factory, a bustling classroom, a courtroom, an orchestra pit or the front seat of a truck.

Ours, after all, is the worker God whose work in creation brought order, provided for every physical need, generated joy, made Eden beautiful, embedded the potential in matter and enabled people to release potential in his creation and in each other. This is the God who created a context for human flourishing. With him. To his glory. And then took a day off.

Good work should do that—and then give us a day off. Future work should do that. To the glory of God.

Disciples for Tomorrow's Workplace

I am convinced that the local church is vital in this. And I am convinced that it is possible to create communities that empower and equip their people for wherever they spend time during the week—including the workplace. I am convinced because I have seen it—in the UK, in the US, in Malaysia. And so have my colleagues and our co-labourers in many other countries. Of course, it is not that the workplace is any more important to God than any other place, but it is a place where God's people spend a lot of time, and it is the place that, historically, churches have found it hardest to disciple people for.

Thirty years ago, churches that discipled people for work were very hard to find. They are still rare but the team I work with at LICC has worked directly with some of them and learned from many of them. More broadly, we have worked across the denominations on a wide variety of disciple-making and workplace initiatives, including with many Anglican dioceses in England, as well as the Church of England's national 'Everyday Faith' initiative, from its conception. And we have worked internationally. This short resource highlights some of what we have learned, specifically as it relates to discipling people for paid work. There is more to learn, of course. But I hope this book will encourage you in your journey of equipping your community to make their contribution to the mission of God in the workplaces of the world.

It is vital that we do.

Following Up

Where to find more on the state and future of work:

- For trends and challenges in work, visit www.lancaster.ac.uk/work-foundation
- D Goodhart, *Head, Hand, Heart: The Struggle for Dignity and Status in the 21st Century* (London: Allen Lane, 2020).

Making it Work for the Whole Church

2

> On the contrary, you must understand now, more clearly, that God is calling you to serve him in and from the ordinary, material and secular activities of human life. He waits for us every day, in the laboratory, in the operating theatre, in the army barracks, in the university chair, in the factory, in the workshop, in the fields, in the home and in all the immense panorama of work.
>
> St Josemaría Escrivá, founder of Opus Dei[5]

Around 40% of people in the UK are in paid employment or actively seeking work. But in most churches in the West, the percentage of the congregation who are in paid work will be significantly lower, simply because of the higher age profile. And that presents challenges for local churches: how do we disciple people in paid work for their contexts whilst not ignoring the needs of the rest of the congregation? How do we integrate an understanding of the challenges of paid work into gathered worship—the preaching, the prayers, the songs? And how do we do it without aggravating the wounds of the jobseekers and the recently redundant?

The first thing to note is that, biblically, pretty much everyone works every day—at least, pretty much everyone over the age of three who is not very severely incapacitated. Everyone, after all, is engaged in some kind of purposeful activity that is of benefit to people and has an impact on God's world. You make a bed and it benefits someone, whether you are doing it for a child at home, or being paid to do it for a patient in a hospital or a guest in a five-star hotel. Biblically, it is all work. And every Christian needs to understand how *their* particular work fits into God's purposes in time and eternity.

Some churches cover paid work as a kind of special interest topic for a season in the way that a church might run a series on the environment or handling conflict. This tends not to bear much long-term fruit, precisely because, as church leader, pioneer mission thinker and LICC Associate the Rev'd Dr Neil Hudson put it:

> Work is not a topic to be addressed but a context to disciple people for.[6]

If we are to enable people to be fruitful for Christ over the long haul, they need a robust biblical understanding of work and vocation. But they also need to be discipled for the challenges and opportunities of contemporary workplaces—the good, the bad and the toxic. Yes, there are obviously distinctive aspects to workplace ministry, but across the denominations, it seems the churches that are good at empowering people for ministry at work tend to be those that are committed to discipling people for *wherever* they spend their time in their Monday-to-Sunday lives, beyond gathered church contexts.

Imagine, for example, a teenager who knows that their maths coursework is significant to God, who knows that practising for their contemporary dance exam and putting the dishes away three days a week can both be done in the power of the Spirit and offered to God in worship. If that is the case, when they get a job in IT, they are only a high kick away from recognizing that their office, like their maths classroom, is a context for mission and ministry.

Truths learnt at one stage of life are transferable to the next.

Similarly, experience gained at one stage of life can be offered to others who are at different stages. A retired manager, for example, may be a mum of three, a nan of four, a neighbour to 20, a friend of 40, a clubmate of 60, a churchgoer with 70, a regular customer in ten shops and a user of all kinds of services. So, yes, a retiree may have a ministry to their peers, but if they understand God's purposes for work they will also be equipped to:

- Encourage and support the missional calling of those in their church who are in paid work.
- Support their adult children (Christian or otherwise) with biblical wisdom and prayer for their workplaces.
- Help their grandchildren (Christian or otherwise) make more biblically informed choices about what work they might be called to.
- Value the work of those who serve them, inevitably enriching the relationship with those people—sanitation workers, postal workers, delivery workers, shop assistants, tradespeople, hairdressers, nail technicians, transport workers, police officers, telephone salespeople, carers, cleaners, doctors…
- Share a gospel that embraces everyday work rather than dismisses it—vital for younger people looking to live an integrated, purposeful life.

Put another way, a rich biblical vision for work and workplace ministry is a key component of fulfilling every Christian's obligation to encourage their sisters and brothers to love and good works (Heb 10.24). And it is a key component of every Christian's calling not only to share a whole-life gospel but to show others how it is lived out, day by working day.

Six Things Every Disciple (Including Workers) Needs to Know

There are things to learn that pertain specifically to the paid workplace and, of course, things to learn that relate to specific job areas. However, the good news is that a big chunk of what workers need to grasp in order to be fruitful in their everyday work is exactly the same as what every disciple of Christ needs to grasp in order to be fruitful in their week.

They need to:

- Know that God is with them right where they are.
- Know that what they do every day really *matters* to God.
- Know *why* their particular work matters to God and how it fits in with his purposes in time and eternity (see p 14).
- Know that fruitfulness for God includes, but is much more than, having evangelistic conversations (see p 12).
- Know how to integrate the issues they face in their Monday-to-Sunday life into their devotional practices (see p 16).
- Know they need other believers to cheer them on in their everyday ministry.

So it is that a church community can contribute a great deal to the fruitfulness of people in paid work without creating a specialist programme, a monthly workers' breakfast, a sermon series, a dedicated home group or missional community—helpful though these can be. Similarly, LICC fieldwork has found that the key convictions and skills that church leaders need to envision and empower fruitful disciples for today's workplace are broadly the same as those needed to make whole-life disciples in general. In sum, seek first to make whole-life disciples, and all these workers will be added unto you.

Following Up

Where to find more on whole-life disciple making:

- N Hudson, *Imagine Church: Releasing Whole-Life Disciples* (Nottingham: IVP, 2007).

- T Cotterell and N Hudson, *Leading a Whole-Life Disciplemaking Church* (Grove Leadership booklet L7).

- M W Goheen and J Mullins, *The Symphony of Mission: Playing Your Part in God's Work in the World* (Grand Rapids, MI: Baker Academic, 2019).

Three Things That Release Workers

3

> God created me to be a plumber. It's perfect for me.
>
> Robert Edwards

Why is it that time and again research has revealed that churches seem to do a much better job helping people in their personal lives, their home lives and their church lives than in their work?

There are all kinds of reasons for this, but at root, the barrier is theological.

The corrosive impact of the sacred-secular divide has, for most of the last two hundred years, affected pretty much every area of church culture. Somehow, we have inadvertently come to live as if life were an orange not a peach. That is, we live as if life were made up of compartmentalized segments, some of which we regard as important to God (church services and activities, social action, evangelism) and some of which we do not (work, rest, leisure, sport, the arts). This is a lie, contradicted again and again through the Scriptures.

Paul, for example, writing to the Colossian Christians, clarifies the scope of Christ's lordship: 'In him all things were created,' 'All things have been created through him and for him.' All things, 'visible and invisible' Col 1.16). Material and non-material. Furthermore, Christ is not only the co-creator of *all* things but the one the Father sent to shed his blood on the cross to reconcile *all* things to himself, to bring peace, wholeness, *shalom* to *all* things (Col 1.20). Christ's goal is nothing less than the renewal and restoration of all things. That is the grand project. And it is into this project that he invites us to participate with our whole lives, including our work. Christ's saving work on the cross does not merely save those who trust in him *from* the penalty of our sins and guarantee resurrection life with him for eternity; it saves us *for* our high calling to work with him in all we do, making his world more like he would want it to be before he returns.

That is why in Colossians Paul can write, 'Whatever you do, work at it with all your heart, as working for the Lord' (Col 3.23). Colossians 3 is built on Colossians 1. After all, everything we do has an impact, for better or worse, on people made in God's image—or on the planet he gave us to steward—or both. All our 'whatevers' matter in God's grand plan. And he weaves them into his 'all.'

Beyond this vital perspective, whilst we can point to many ways that workers have been fruitfully discipled, three things seem to have had a consistently high impact on the confidence and fruitfulness of workers:

- They have a rich framework for fruitfulness at work.
- They know why *their* particular work matters to God.
- They integrate work issues into their devotional life.

Finding a Framework for Fruitfulness

Many Christians believe that, if you are not in church-paid work, there are only really three main ways to please God:

- Volunteer in the local church.
- Be involved in some direct service of the poor.
- Be engaged in evangelistic activity.

This narrowness in the understanding of what fruitfulness looks like seems to apply almost whatever someone's job is—from cleaning to graphic design, from shelf-stacking to engineering. It even applies to people doing jobs that, because they involve care and nurture, tend to have a higher status in the Christian subculture. So, for example, there was the psychotherapist who was weeping as she wondered whether to change jobs because there was no legal way to take the initiative to share the gospel in her consultations. Never mind the fact that she had contributed to the mental, emotional and relational well-being of hundreds of people, and thereby blessed their families and friends and schools and workplaces. No, somehow that did not count. Evangelism was her only criterion for fruitfulness.

Similarly, there was the head teacher who, by the age of 34, had turned around two failing primary schools in East Glasgow but who did not think she had done anything significant for God. Never mind the fact that she had improved the lives of hundreds of children, given hope to their parents, guardians and carers, and lifted the morale of two whole communities.

Workers need a rich framework for fruitfulness that includes evangelism but does not make evangelism what it is not—the only or supreme mark of fruitfulness.

All fruitfulness comes from abiding in Christ. He is the vine, we are the branches (John 15). And just as an apple tree produces apples and a pear tree produces pears, so a Christ-vine produces fruit that reflects Christ's character, ways and purposes. Here is a framework that tries to capture some of the scope of what that might look like: the 6Ms.[7]

It asks us to consider how, in and through our work, we might:

- Model godly character.
- Make good work.
- Minister grace and love.
- Mould the culture.
- Be Mouthpieces for truth and justice.
- Be Messengers of the gospel.

The 6Ms and the Plumber
Well, what does that look like for a plumber?

In terms of modelling godly character, my friend Robert trades in bringing peace: the water may be gushing down the walls, the bedroom ceiling may be about to land on the kitchen table, but he walks in calmly: 'It's going to be okay.'

He makes good work. He gets there on time, looks for the best long-term solution, not just the quick fix. When he discovers some hodge-podge of dodgy temporary connections under the floorboards, he will let the customer know. And he always leaves everything clean and dry.

Robert gets to minister grace and love, sometimes doing a boiler service for free for a customer in trouble so they do not lose their warranty. And he is always trying to pick up on people's interests, their mood. Are they lonely? Are they sick? Can I sow some joy? Offer a word of encouragement?

How does Robert mould the culture? Well, you cannot change the culture in a family by changing the washers on a tap, but Robert has moulded a culture of tremendous trust over time. People leave him their keys and go out for the day, and they recommend him to their friends. So when he tells a customer that the hodge-podge of temporary connections needs addressing, they do not think he is inventing work to increase his income. They know he has their best interests at heart.

He is a mouthpiece of truth and justice. He will say 'No' to working for landlords who do not do the right thing for their tenants. He will say 'No' to doing jobs for cash for a client who wants to save the VAT. He will not charge a big, fat call-out fee for a job that took him two minutes in a house that was on his way to his next job.

And, yes, he is a messenger for the gospel, telling people about his church and the difference Jesus makes to him in his own calm, matter-of-fact, generous way.

The thing about the 6Ms is this: pretty much anyone who works with someone probably has an opportunity to do five of them every single working day.

Every day we have the opportunity to allow the Lord to ripen the fruit of the Spirit in us: love, joy, peace, forbearance, kindness, goodness, faithfulness, gentleness and self-control. Every day people get to do good work, show love and grace, mould the culture around them and tell the truth. And that is true however grim the work itself might be. After all, many of God's people are in work that they do not particularly enjoy, in physical conditions that may be difficult or dangerous, or among colleagues that they do not trust or like much, or in market conditions that have made everyone worried that they might not have a job next month, next week, tomorrow.

Whatever the conditions, the 6Ms do not just give people a sense of how they might be able to bear fruit in the future—they help people see that God has *already* been at work in their lives, that they have *already* been fruitful. And that builds their confidence that God could work even more powerfully. Furthermore, the 6Ms help workers realize that they have a rich testimony of how God has worked in their lives, beyond the testimony of how they came to faith. God is alive in their lives now. God makes a difference in their work now. There is so much more to share with colleagues.

Knowing Why Your Particular Work Matters to God

This is the second thing that makes a huge difference to the confidence of workers. It is one thing to know that work in general is important to God (Gen 2.15), that we are meant to be engaged in productive activity six days a week (Exod 20.9), that we can do whatever we do wholeheartedly for God (Col 3.23–24). But it is quite another to believe that *my* particular work matters to God. Sweeping streets, washing dishes, selling cars, running a small business, dancing to the glory of God? Why might any of that matter to the king of the universe?

In addressing this issue, I have found it helpful to bring together Colossians 1 and the mission of God (outlined earlier) with an exploration of God's purposes for work in Genesis 1 and 2.

The Worker God at Work

Why does God create Adam and Eve on day six? Why wait? Why not create humanity on day one?

Because if God had created humans on day one it would have been dark and there would have been nowhere to stand. By the time God creates Adam and Eve he has made everything ready. There is ground to stand on, air to breathe, a gorgeous environment to enjoy, delicious, nutritious food to eat, water to drink, animals to look after and purposeful work to be done in the garden.

What has God done? God has created a context for the flourishing of human-kind and, indeed, all creation.

God is love and everything he does is an expression of his love, so of course he wants to create a context in which human beings can flourish. It is what people—single, married, with or without children—do when they make a home. They try to create a place where they and their friends can come and relax and rest and be refreshed. A place of flourishing.

It is what a good manager does. They try to create a context in which people can do good work in a good way. As one manager put it to me: 'My job is to roll the rocks off the runway so other people can fly.'

It is what good church leaders do—try to create an environment in which people can flourish as whole human beings in Christ.

As we look at what seem to be the aims of God's work, here are five factors from Genesis 1 and 2 for workers to reflect on:

God Brings Order
In this case, out of chaos (Gen 1.2). How do people's jobs bring order? Tidying, maintaining, servicing, planning, policing…

God's Work Provides
Food, water, a secure environment. How do people's jobs provide for themselves and others? For some it is by starting businesses that create work for others. Sarah co-ran a business with 400 employees. She did not think her work was at all significant to God until she realized that he is not just pleased with those who work hard to *alleviate* poverty to his glory—he is pleased with those who work hard to *prevent* poverty in the first place, to his glory. And her business had provided 400 people with good work, and an extraordinarily positive, caring environment in which to do it.

God's Work Brings Joy
God created a garden of 'delight' ('Eden' in Hebrew). 'And the trees were pleasing to the eye and good for food' (Gen 2.9).

Lots of work brings joy. There is the joy in a well-prepared, simple meal: hot, fluffy scrambled eggs on crunchy sourdough toast with fresh-ground black pepper. There is joy in a well-made bed—pleasing to the eye and inviting to get into. There is joy in bringing joy to oth-ers—fixing the leak, rewiring a house, or developing a product that

---

means you do not have to spend ten minutes scraping the limescale off a tap with your newly manicured nails. Thank you, Mr Muscle. And there is joy in a well-designed form, or a clear set of instructions, or in any system that just works well.

God's Work Brings Beauty
God *sees* all his work as 'very good' (Gen 1.31), with the implication in this context of aesthetic as well as functional excellence. In addition, specific elements are highlighted as 'pleasing to the eye'—the trees (Gen 2.9) and the fruit (Gen 3.6).

People bring beauty to a myriad of everyday tasks. There can be beauty in the way biscuits are arranged on a plate. Or in choosing the right shade of cerulean for the cushions on the fuchsia sofa. And, of course, beauty is not just visual. There is beauty in a well-crafted sentence, in the shimmy that takes a footballer past a defender and, for some, in the elegance and harmonious resolution of an equation like Euler's Identity: $e^{i\pi} + 1 = 0$.

And there is work that preserves beauty, like the good work of the Hillingdon London Borough Council sanitation team who collect our rubbish every Monday and always leave things so tidy.

God's Work Releases Potential
In matter. In human beings. God creates matter. Matter matters. And he releases its potential in an almost infinite variety of forms.

And as God tends and nurtures us, so we can do the same for others and for creation: seed to sapling to tree to fruit to apple pie; cooing infant to talking toddler to teenage debater to local MP; sand to sandcastles, or glass, or silicon chips, or abrasive cleaning systems.

Of course, not every job will necessarily fulfil all five aspects and not everyone will be able to see instantly how their work aligns with God's goals for work. So, as ever, it may take some teasing out, either one-on-one or in groups. But when people see how their work is a continuation of God's, then the sense of meaningful purpose is invigorating. The alternative is to consign people to the crushing burden of futility.

Integrating Work Issues into Your 'Devotional Life'
The third key characteristic of fruitful workplace disciples is that they integrate work issues into their devotional life. Of course, if something is important to you then you talk to God about it. And when you do, he is very likely to talk back and to get even more involved. Still, in the context of an overall church

culture where interest in, teaching on, and prayer for work is likely to have been a rarity for most of people's lives, it is not to be taken for granted. Recent experiments in pioneer churches, as well as anecdotal evidence, suggest that it is vital to help people integrate their everyday activities beyond the church into the way they engage with God—whether Bible reading, or prayer, or reflection, or habits and practices that serve to create a conscious engagement of daily life with Christ.

It could be discussing work issues with a prayer partner, it could be belonging to a small group where frontline and work concerns are part of the culture, it could be always praying for their work when they drive past the oak tree by the builder's merchants on the A71, or asking the Lord 'to establish the work of their hands' every time they wash them (Ps 90.17).

So one of the ways to nurture workplace disciples is to encourage them to integrate workplace concerns into their own prayer lives. And one of the ways to begin that is to integrate workplace concerns into the church's corporate praying.

Following Up

Explore LICC's range of resources for equipping workers at licc.org.uk/work

The 6Ms

- M Greene, *Fruitfulness on the Frontline* (Nottingham: IVP, 2014).
- M Greene, *Fruitfulness on the Frontline*, DVD Group Resource (London: LICC, 2014).

Theology of Work

- T Keller and K L Alsdorf, *Every Good Endeavour* (London: Hodder and Stoughton, 2014).
- M Kaemingk and C B Willson, *Work and Worship: Reconnecting Our Labor and Liturgy* (Grand Rapids, MI: Baker Academic, 2020).
- Pope John Paul II, *Laborem Exercens* (Vatican: Libreria Editrice Vaticana, 1981). Available at: www.vatican.va (search for *laborem exercens*)

Vocation

- *Kingdom Calling*, www.churchofengland.org/our-faith/your-calling

Ministry at Work

- M Greene, *Thank God It's Monday* (Edinburgh: Muddy Pearl, fifth edition, 2019).

- M Greene, R Walker, C Hippsley, D Leeds, *Transforming Work—Discipleship for the Workplace*; 8-part group discipleship journey (London: LICC, 2018). Available at: https://licc.org.uk/tw

Workplace Evangelism

- B Peel and W Larrimore, *Workplace Grace: Becoming a Spiritual Influence at Work* (Longview, TX: LeTourneau, 2014).

Seven Ways for Leaders to Help

4

> Well, it's not that he (the vicar) preaches or teaches a lot on work. It's rather that there always seems to be something in the service that affirms—in however small a way—my role as a worker. It could be a snippet of a prayer or an illustration, but there's always something.
>
> Gill Dandy, PR Consultant

Discipling people for the workplace does not involve turning every Sunday service into a workplace seminar. Rather, like the vicar above, it means integrating whole-life mission, including the workplace, into the way things are done. Integration is the means; theological conviction is the fuel.

Indeed, the leaders who seem to be most effective in discipling workers do not seem to be smarter, harder working, more prayerful, or holier than those that are not so effective. But there are some distinctives. The first one will not come as a shock.

Believing that Work, Workers and the Workplace All Matter to God

Everything follows from that. They are deeply convinced that work matters to God and that it is a critical arena for mission and discipleship. That is, they believe that God will not only seek to work *through* his people in the workplace, but that he will work *in* them. The workplace is not only a context in which to make disciples, it is also a context in which to *grow* as a disciple. Effective disciple makers seek to help people see that God will use the challenges they encounter to grow them in character, to prompt them to pray, to increase their dependence on him for wisdom, to heighten their alertness to his presence and action, and to continue pursuing his mission there—in good times and hard times.

Being Curious About People's Everyday Lives

They find a way to listen and proactively look for ways to find out about people's work and their lives beyond the gathered church. This is not necessarily about adding something to a minister's to-do list, but rather, expanding the scope of the conversations and interactions they already have to include a concern for people's work. It can be as simple as:

- Using the time after a service to talk to at least one person about their week, beyond church activities.

- Piggybacking a question about work or the school gate or their football team onto the end of a text or a WhatsApp or an email about the songs for next week, or the flower rota, or the window repair.

Visiting People at Work

This is the practice that ministers report has had the most impact on their understanding and enabling of the scattered ministry of God's people. The benefits are myriad:

- *You learn a lot.* You see the context, you feel the atmosphere, you get a sense of the kind of people who are there. You ask questions. And the questions trigger a wealth of information you would not otherwise get. 'That's Sunita, my boss I've been telling you about. That's Amal who we've been praying for. Oh, and an amazing thing happened last month.' And, vitally, you discover over time that every workplace is a foreign country and that they are all different. Their cultures are different, their morale is different, their spiritual openness is different—some are wonderful, some are OK, some are grim. And that means every disciple needs to discern how God would have them live and share the good news in their context.

- *You encourage people immensely.* A visit sends a powerful message to your church member. They matter. This place matters. And it can change the way *they* see their context and their ministry. 'What am I doing here? What am I praying for? Who am I praying for?' Visits also send a powerful message to your congregation. You cannot visit everyone, but everyone will hear about it and will understand that their work, too, matters to God.

- *You minister differently afterwards.* What you learn not only gives you pastoral and missional insight, it enables you to shape teaching and training that better fit the contexts the congregation are in, and it often provides fuel for sermon applications and illustrations.

Of course, a visit—whether or not you are wearing a collar (always good to ask how to dress)—can catalyze a new phase of purposeful spiritual engagement in the worker's ministry. One man met his dog-collared vicar in reception and said to him, 'They don't know I'm a Christian here.' The minister replied, 'How are we going to handle that?' The reply came: 'They're about to find out.'

The point is that, however you do it, it is vital to have regular practices that enable you to find out about people's working lives. And, if you are a church leader, it is important that your team does the same. It is hard to equip people effectively for a mission field that you know very little about. One church made it mandatory for the three church-paid workers to visit someone's frontline every Wednesday. One rector made it a priority for his curates to visit someone in their workplace every week for their entire curacy. Once every six weeks is usually fine to achieve the key goals: a shift in consciousness, and a steady growth in understanding. But once you start, you will probably want to do more.

Consistently Connecting the Bible with People's Contexts, and Helping Them Do the Same

Workplace visits help to enrich how preachers and teachers approach the Scriptures and apply them to everyday contexts.

So, for example, you visit the Cherry Tree Bakery in Burnley, England. Gary, the owner, walks you around and tells you that a high proportion of his workforce are from eastern Europe and not hugely welcomed by many people in the town. They are far from home, living in crowded digs to save money, some of which they can then send home. He tells you that he wants his company to be a safe place for them. The word he uses is 'sanctuary.' And because he wants to honour his employees, the canteen is beautifully decorated and furnished with leather chairs, and the loos are more like what you would expect in a four-star hotel than in an industrial unit on the edge of town. Now suppose, just suppose, that you are preaching through Ruth. Well, the connections come flooding in: there is Ruth, a foreigner doing a low-paid job in a not altogether welcoming environment, and doing it well. There is Boaz, the landowner, proactively seeking to bless Ruth—to protect her from harassment, to ensure she has water throughout the day (Ruth 2.9) and food at lunchtime (Ruth 2.14).

And you can make the connections not only for the congregation but for Gary, the owner, who has perhaps not seen the parallels between the kind of culture he is trying to create for his workers and the kind of culture that Boaz was trying to create for Ruth. And he would be encouraged by that realization.

Indeed, one of the great gifts preachers can give their worker-hearers is the ability to make the biblical connections to their daily work for themselves. And connections abound because so much of the Bible is either directly about work, or set in a working context, or applicable to work. Indeed, following the lectionary would provide more than enough grist for workplace nourishment.

Consistently Sharing Stories of What Fruitfulness Looks Like in Everyday Life, Including Work

The vast majority of Christians are much more fruitful in and for Christ than they think they are. And one of the ways to help them see that is to tell the stories of how God has been working in other people's lives. The plumber who brings peace to his clients (as well as water running in the right places). The armed protection officer who taught his colleagues Jesus' way of forgiveness at No 10 Downing Street. The hotel manager who opened a jammed safe through prayer. The bus driver who is a 'chaplain' to her regulars. The binman who gets given prayer requests. The checkout attendant who customers are prepared to queue longer for because he is genuinely interested in them…

Of course, the most powerful stories are the ones that come out of the congregation you are in. Indeed, once people know that you are interested in their testimonies, they will begin to realize that they too have a story like that and share it with you. Stories beget stories. Which leads to one of the other key characteristics of churches that disciple workers well.

Enlisting Other People in the Cause

Champions, story-collectors, story-sharers, encouragers.

Paulina worked in finance. She noticed that her senior church minister did not seem to have any workplace stories to share in sermons, so she took the initiative to share hers. And he would store them away and bring them out, as appropriate.

Peter, a man in financial services in my previous church, regularly brought me articles about trends in work, management, HR and so on. Hugely helpful.

Ian, a food marketeer, found out about This Time Tomorrow.[8] TTT is a three-to-five-minute interview in a church service about where someone will be 'this time tomorrow': their work or some non-church activity, such as the school gate, the gym, a walking group. Who are you? What do you do? What are the challenges and opportunities? How can we pray?

Ian floated the idea with his vicar and offered to find people for a monthly slot, identify the things that might be most helpful to the congregation, and then brief the minister who, in this case, did the interviews.

TTT honours the interviewees. It reinforces the importance of everyday mission to the congregation, it sparks the imagination, it triggers everyday life conversations in the congregation, and it enriches relationships. Church leaders across the denominations consistently say that TTT was the single most impactful action they took in *beginning* to help a whole congregation see the significance of their day-to-day lives.

Who might you enlist to help fuel everyday mission through your congregation?

Signposting Workers to Resources, Courses and Potential Mentors

The first year it happened, we at LICC thought it was just one of those things: two people coming on the same weekend workplace residential from the same church. The second year, we had another three from the same church. And the year after that, two more. This surely was not happening by chance. And indeed it was not. The minister had proactively recommended the course to prayerfully-selected people in his church. And they came. And pretty soon those who came started to run work-related courses in the church. And then they got together with others from the same city (Nottingham) who had also been on the course, and together began to take wider cross-denominational initiatives in the area. But it began with one minister looking out for ways to help people keep on developing. And he, as it has turned out, was not the only minister doing it, nor LICC the only place people were being signposted to.

Every church leader can lay good foundations for workplace ministry, but no church leader can hope to resource everyone in their congregation for the huge range of issues that contemporary work raises. And you do not need to. There is wisdom in the wider church body both nationally and internationally (see licc.org.uk for resources.)

Those are just seven characteristics but, at root, consciousness is the key: the consciousness that God has a purpose for his people in their everyday lives and is very likely to already be working in and through them, right where they are.

Once leaders are convinced of that, it becomes relatively easy to see all kinds of opportunities to integrate everyday discipling into what you already do in worship services, small groups and beyond.

Following Up

- For a guide to workplace visits and how to tell their stories, see: https://licc.org.uk/workplace-visits and https://churchofengland.org/everyday-faith https://licc.org.uk/unearthing-stories

- For This Time Tomorrow, six key practices, and how to tell stories, see: https://www.churchofengland.org/our-faith/everyday-faith

5 Getting Sunday into Monday

Integrating everyday discipleship into the culture of a local church is not primarily about doing *new* things but about doing things, you already do in a new way. And in that regard, almost any component of church life can contribute.

Shaping Sunday Services

Take a Sunday service. People will be greeted, songs will be sung, prayers prayed, a sermon delivered, perhaps holy communion served, and then people will be dismissed.

Might some of the songs reflect God's concern for every area of life, for the various spheres of society, for the *shalom* of the nation, or the city, town, village, or area of which God has made this community a part? Might some of the visuals on the PowerPoint slides, if you use them, be of the places that people find themselves in the week? Might the words of *Be Thou My Vision* not be laid out over a mountain view or a sunset but over a picture of the local industrial estate, the high street, the dishes in someone's kitchen sink, the local pub...?

Might the prayers include an awareness of the local economy, the jobs people do, and the particular pressures people face at different times of the year? Sheep farmers at lambing season, accountants in March and April, teachers in the run-up to Christmas and exams, cab drivers round big holidays, schoolchildren and students in September...?

Might the sermon be alert to how the lectionary reading or the chosen Bible passage addresses work directly, might apply to work, or is set in a working context? Naaman's wife's unnamed servant girl in 2 Kings 5, Paul in the boat in Acts 27, Ruth in Boaz's field, the accounts of David's working life in 1 and 2 Samuel and, of course, the 53 psalms in which he mentions the enemies he faces in his work? Might the stories and illustrations encompass a broader range of arenas, including the workplace?

Similarly, an everyday-faith consciousness might change the way you open a service—not, as sometimes happens, inviting people to lay down all that has happened to them in the week at the door, but to bring all that they have experienced in their week to the community of Christ, to name it and lay it down at the foot of the cross.

You may not be in the Anglican liturgical tradition, but it offers a rich example of how whole-life consciousness can be woven into Sunday's liturgy, even if currently it is not necessarily understood in that way. Indeed, one Anglican vicar who had been involved with LICC in a disciple-making hub commented on the words of dismissal:

> The strongest effect on me personally (of the process) has been a new sense of the implications of the words, 'Go in peace to love and serve the Lord.'

I wonder what is in our hearts and heads when we say or hear those words before the congregation scatters?

For me, those words work in two directions. First, they point outwards: 'Go and love and serve out there.' But they also point back to the service: 'On the basis of all that we have done together—welcome and praise, confession and creed, intercession and offertory, word and sacrament—on the basis of the *shalom* we have received in Christ, and the *shalom* that we have enjoyed with one another, now go in peace to love and serve the Lord…out there.' Once those words are understood as embracing all of life, all of the tasks and challenges and encounters of the coming week, then they imply that what has just happened in the service will indeed serve to provide perspective, wisdom and strength for all those contexts.

A concern for the 'sent' life of the people of God does not diminish the importance of its gathered life. It increases it. Our gathering together must minister to all that we have borne, and fuel us for all we are to face as we live and share the good news right where we are.

But I doubt that the vast majority of God's people hear the words of dismissal and think that it includes cooking a meal (whether at home or in a restaurant), digging a hole (whether at home or on the M6), or almost any of the work they will do in the coming week. But once people understand that all their life matters then those words are very likely to reinforce that perspective. We do not need to change the words. We just need to ensure they are rightly understood.

And the same applies to holy communion. Here is how one worshipper responded during a service:

> At church this week I was asked to take part in the offertory procession and so I took the box of wafers up, and my friend took the wine, as the sidespeople took up the collection. Because I was near the altar I could hear the prayers over the gifts that the priest was saying, whilst the rest of the congregation sang. She said of the wine, 'Fruit of the

> vine and work of human hands' and I noticed my own hands at that moment, and thought about the work they do. Throughout the week, I have been drawn back to that moment whenever I catch sight of my hands working. Mostly, they are doing that on a keyboard as I type emails. It's helping me think about my work as coming from God, and an offering to God.

Of course, different traditions use different liturgies, but all refer to the bread and the wine. Some make explicit the reality that Jesus took bread 'made by human hands' and wine 'made by human hands.' That is, that Christ took something that human beings worked to produce and transformed it. Of course, it took many hands to produce the bread: the ploughman, the sower, the reaper, the fermenter of yeast and the baker. And many hands too to produce the wine. Indeed, what is implicit in the sacrament is made explicit elsewhere—whatever we do can be done for the Lord, whatever we do can glorify his name, whatever we do can be a sign to others of his kingship, whatever we offer can become something more (Col 3.17, 23–24). A widow's mite becomes an object lesson in generosity (Luke 21.1–4); a pint of nard a signpost of the supreme value of Christ (John 12.1–8); an act of obedience the trigger for a huge catch of fish and deep repentance (Luke 5.1–11).

Using the Church Year

You can see the same potential to engage with everyday life in the Anglican church year, which of course can be imitated by any denomination without using the same words. After all, the church year tracks with the economic year. Plough Sunday is followed by Rogation Sunday is followed by Harvest. Most churches will celebrate Harvest, often broadening it out from the display of agricultural produce to include objects that reflect the many ways in which God provides for his people—a mop, a laptop, a stethoscope, a brick and, on one altar, an unemployment benefit form.

However, if we only celebrate Harvest, we miss the opportunity to communicate that God wants to be involved in every phase of the work. Plough Sunday, falling early in January, is an opportunity to dedicate the work of the coming year to the Lord, and to express gratitude for the tools and technologies that enable it. One Baptist church I know does exactly that each year in a service complete with plough, so that everyone can dedicate to God their work on all their frontlines beyond the church: workplaces, places they volunteer, activities they engage in with people who do not know Jesus—book clubs, camera clubs, football teams…

Similarly, if you live in inner-city Liverpool, you probably will not walk the parish bounds on Rogation Sunday to ask God's blessing on the wheat seed that is about to be sown. But it is an opportunity to pray the Lord's blessing on all the economic activity of the people in your area and beyond. One minister I met used to go into the businesses on the high street and ask the managers or owners how she and the church might pray for them.

Looking more broadly at the gathered life of the church, small groups tend to be vital to creating a whole-life disciple-making culture. Certainly there are lots of resources designed for people in paid employment. But most groups include a variety of people, so the key is to maintain the group's focus on *everyone's* opportunities to engage in mission beyond gathered church activities. At LICC we use the word 'frontline' as shorthand for that. Others use 'everyday faith,' or 'scattered saints,' or 'ambassadors.' What matters most is that members of the group support each other's growth in fruitfulness for Christ in the world through prayer, wisdom-sharing, skill development and encouragement. And critical to that is ensuring that the prayer life of the group does not end up only focusing on pressure points and crises, losing sight of why God's people go to work and the vital contribution they have to make to his mission there.

For it is indeed a joyous truth that every day, God sends his people into his world to be:

> ...channels of his blessing, vessels of his presence, stewards of his planet, sources of his wisdom, models of his ways, sharers of his truth, lavishers of his love—for the sake of the work, the workers, the workplaces, and the communities they serve. To the glory of the Creator and Redeemer of all things.

May it be so.

Following Up

- A Billington and N Hudson, *Whole-Life Preaching*, video course. See: https://licc.org.uk/preaching
- S and S Hargreaves, *Whole-Life Worship* (London: IVP, 2017).
- S and S Hargreaves, *Whole-Life Worship Journey Pack* (London: LICC, 2017). See: https://licc.org.uk/worship
- *Frontline Sundays*—service ideas to begin the disciple-making journey, licc.org.uk/frontlinesundays

Notes

1 Josemaría Escrivá, *Conversations with Monsignor Escrivá de Balaguer*, Nos 113 and 54 (New York: Scepter, 1968).

2 Sister Wendy Beckett, *Desert Island Discs*, BBC Radio 4, 16 December 2012

3 https://www.lifelinechurch.co.uk/two-minute-testimonies/oleh/

4 *D Sayers*, Letters to a Diminished Church (Nashville, TN: Thomas Nelson, 2004) p138.

5 Josemaría Escrivá, *Conversations with Monsignor Escrivá de Balaguer*, No 114 (New York: Scepter, 1968).

6 Neil Hudson live in LICC, *Imagine Church* Training Events, 2010–2019

7 LICC, 'The 6Ms – Uncovering Fruitfulness Where You Are', https://licc.org.uk/resources/6ms/

8 LICC, 'This Time Tomorrow', https://licc.org.uk/resources/this-time-tomorrow/